BON

AH! QU'IL EST LE BON DIEU

*Ex Libris*
*Notre Dame High School*
*San Jose*

# LET'S VISIT NORTH AFRICA

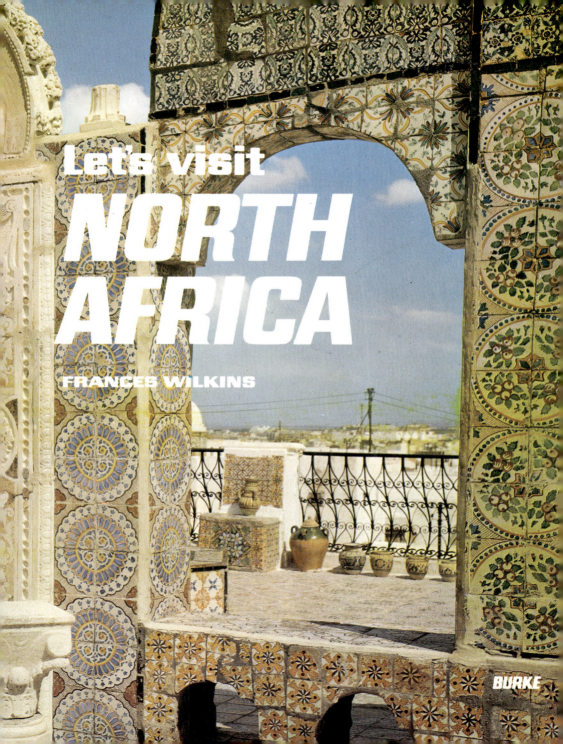

# Let's visit
# NORTH AFRICA

FRANCES WILKINS

BURKE

First published September 1979
Second revised edition 1983
© Frances Wilkins 1970 and 1983

## ACKNOWLEDGEMENTS

The Author and Publishers are grateful to the following individuals and organizations for permission to reproduce illustrations in this book:

Air France; Camera Press Ltd.; J. Allan Cash; Colour Library International; Douglas Dickins; Esso Petroleum Co. Ltd.; A. F. Kersting; Keystone Press Agency Ltd.; Monitor Press Features; Office National Marocain du Tourisme; Tunisian Trade Office; N. Vincent.

The cover picture of the Bab Boujeloud in Fez is reproduced by kind permission of J. Allan Cash.

**CIP data**

Wilkins, Frances
    Let's visit North Africa. – 2nd ed.
    1.  Africa, North – Social life and customs –
Juvenile literature
    I.  Title
    960'.3    DT30
    ISBN 0 222 00917 9

Burke Publishing Company Limited
Pegasus House, 116–120 Golden Lane, London EC1Y 0TL, England.
Burke Publishing (Canada) Limited
Toronto, Ontario, Canada.
Burke Publishing Company Inc.
540 Barnum Avenue, Bridgeport, Connecticut 06608, U.S.A.
Filmset in 'Monophoto' Baskerville by Green Gates Studios, Hull, England.
Printed in Singapore by Tien Wah Press (Pte) Ltd.

15278

# Contents

M E D I T

Bizerta
Tunis

Algiers
Oran
KABYLIA MTS
Constantine
Kairo

Gafsa

Tangier
Tetuan
Chaouen
RIF MTS
Rabat
Salé
Fez
Casablanca
Meknes
MIDDLE ATLAS

Nefta
Tozeur
Gabès
Ma

TUNIS

MOROCCO

Marrakesh

HIGH ATLAS

ANTI ATLAS

TRANS SAHARA MOTOR ROAD

A L G E R I A

S A H A R A

TRANS SAHARA MOTOR ROAD

# NORTH AFRICA

DESERT AREA ||||||||||||||||||||||||||||||||||||||

0  20 40 60 80 100    150      200     250
STATUTE MILES
0    50  100 150 200 250 300 350 400
KILOMETRES

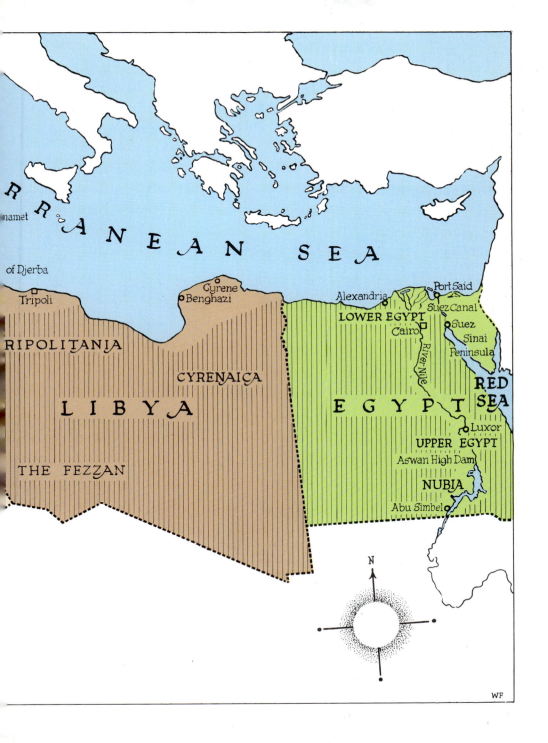

MEDITERRANEAN SEA

namet

of Djerba

Tripoli

TRIPOLITANIA

CYRENAICA

Cyrene
Benghazi

LIBYA

THE FEZZAN

Alexandria

Port Said

Suez Canal

LOWER EGYPT

Cairo

Suez

Sinai
Peninsula

River Nile

EGYPT

RED
SEA

Luxor

UPPER EGYPT

Aswan High Dam

NUBIA

Abu Simbel

N

WF

Date palms form the background to this typical oasis scene

# The Land and the People

When we speak of North Africa we are usually referring to five neighbouring countries—Morocco, Tunisia, Algeria, Libya and Egypt. The Mediterranean Sea forms the northern border of all of them. Morocco also has a long coastline on the Atlantic Ocean.

In many ways these five countries are quite different from each other. For instance, Algeria is larger than the whole of western Europe, while Tunisia is barely the size of England and Wales. But they all have one outstanding feature in common— in the south they all form part of the vast desert known as the Sahara.

It is difficult to live in the sandy wastes of the desert. There is very little water and, as a result, hardly anything will grow there. For this reason, the great majority of people in North Africa live near the sea. This is the region where the rainfall is highest and so the land is most fertile.

There is one important exception to this. In Egypt, practically the entire population is crowded into a narrow strip of land along the banks of the River Nile. Without the Nile virtually the whole of Egypt would be desert; but with careful irrigation the Nile can be used to make the land on either side of it very fertile indeed.

There are also some people in North Africa who live near the oases. The word "oasis" is used to describe any place, small or large, where there is water in the desert. A small oasis may be just two or three date palms and a few bushes around a well. On the other hand, there is one oasis in Tunisia which has some 700,000 palms and is watered by nearly 200 springs.

The most mountainous country of North Africa is Morocco. In northern Morocco there are the Rif Mountains, and further south there are three separate ranges of the Atlas Mountains. The highest of these, called the High Atlas, rises to well over 13,000 feet (3,960 metres). The Atlas Mountains also extend across Algeria to Tunisia, but they gradually become lower towards the east.

In the coastal regions of North Africa the climate is mainly Mediterranean. This means that the summers are warm and dry, and the winters are cool and wet. In the desert areas of the south, however, the temperature in summer often reaches 120° Fahrenheit (49° Centigrade) or more in the shade. Even in winter, the midday temperature rarely drops below 70° Fahrenheit (21° Centigrade).

In North Africa only the mountain areas have snow. In winter, the snow is so deep there that wealthy North Africans can enjoy winter sports. The mountains are also popular for holidays in the summer. Many people go there to escape the stifling heat of the plains.

The western and central part of North Africa is sometimes known as "Barbary". (There are many traditional stories about Barbary pirates.) Originally, the word Barbary meant "the land of the barbarians". "Barbarians" was the name the Romans gave to the people they found living in this part of

10

**A Berber band**

North Africa. The descendants of these "barbarians" are now called Berbers. They make up nearly half the population of Morocco and Libya, and about one third of the population of Algeria. There is also a small number of Berbers living in Tunisia, but no one knows exactly how many. There are few, if any, living in Egypt, however.

Apart from the Berbers, nearly all present-day North Africans are Arabs. They are the descendants of the war-like hordes from the Middle East who overran North Africa in the seventh century after Christ. Generally speaking, the Arabs have darker skins than the Berbers. They are not a tall race, but they are often very muscular and wiry.

There is little intermingling between the Berbers and the

11

Arabs. They do not like or trust each other, and their ways of life are very different.

Most of the Berbers make their living by farming. Many of them still live in the same small villages where their families have lived for generations. Their homes are one-roomed huts, made of bricks dried in the sun. There is hardly any furniture, for the Berbers sit on the floor to eat or work.

The Arabs, on the other hand, were originally a nomadic people. They wandered from place to place looking for fresh pasture for their herds. There are still some Arabs living like this, on the edge of the desert. We call them bedouin. But they are not typical of the majority of Arabs today.

Most present-day Arabs are town-dwellers. They form by far the larger part of the inhabitants of every North African city. If an Arab is rich, he likes to live in much the same kind of home as a European does, complete with a television set and a washing-machine.

In Egypt, however, the situation is different. Practically all the Egyptians are Arabs, including those who are employed on the land. These agricultural workers are known as *fellahs*, or *fellahin*. They live in very primitive conditions, and are regarded with contempt by the rest of the population.

The official language of all the North African countries is Arabic. It is a semitic language, which means that it is similar to Aramaic, the language spoken by Jesus.

*Spoken* Arabic varies a little from country to country. Even so, most North Africans can follow each other's speech where-ever they happen to live. *Written* Arabic is exactly the same everywhere. There are twenty-eight characters in the Arabic alphabet and, unlike our own language, it is written from right to left. To English eyes written Arabic looks rather like shorthand. But it can be written so gracefully that it has been used for centuries to decorate such things as prayer-mats, wall-tiles and ceilings.

## *Ancient Times*

The earliest inhabitants of North Africa lived a wandering life. They were always moving from place to place looking for fresh hunting- or grazing-grounds. Then some of them decided to settle down in the Nile Valley. They chose this area because they had noticed a curious geographical fact.

Once a year the Nile bursts its banks and floods the land on either side of it. Later it subsides and leaves behind it a thick layer of fertile mud. The people had only to scatter their seeds and leave the rest to the hot sunshine. For a few weeks' work they could expect to reap a rich harvest.

It seemed an ideal place for these early people to settle. But they soon discovered that the Nile does not behave in exactly the same way each year. The river sometimes rose so little that the crops withered and the people starved. In other years the water rose so high that whole villages were swept away and the inhabitants were drowned.

These disasters led the more intelligent people to try to control the River Nile. They began studying ways of channelling the water and digging an irrigation system. Then some of them realized that they needed records of the changes in water-level. So they gradually developed a simple form of writing, called pictograms, and invented a calendar.

The struggle to master the Nile took place long before the country now called Egypt existed. But it undoubtedly laid the foundations for the great Egyptian civilization. This began in 3200 B.C., when the whole of Egypt was united under King Menes. He was the first of a long line of kings, or pharaohs, who ruled Egypt for nearly three thousand years.

The most famous of the pharaohs is probably King Cheops. He came to the throne in 2590 B.C., and under his guidance the country became rich and powerful. He built the Great Pyramid, which still stands near the modern city of Cairo. It is the only one of the Seven Wonders of the World which still exists.

Another pharaoh, whose name is famous, was King Tutankhamon. He came to the throne as a boy in the year 1360 B.C. (It is worth remembering that King Menes would have seemed as ancient to King Tutankhamon as Julius Caesar does to us. This gives you some idea of how long the Egyptian civilization lasted.)

**One of the famous pyramids just outside Cairo**

In 1923 an English archaeologist named Howard Carter opened the tomb of King Tutankhamon. Inside he found all the dead king's most treasured possessions. When the king died, his friends placed them there because they thought he would need them in the After Life. Most of these beautiful and fascinating objects can now be seen in the Cairo Museum.

The Egyptian civilization began to decline round about 700 B.C. Egypt was first plundered by the Assyrians, and then conquered by the Persians. It also fell to the Macedonians in 332 B.C.; but the Macedonians were such weak rulers that the country slowly came under Egyptian influence once again.

During the great days of the Egyptian civilization the rest of North Africa was inhabited mainly by the Berbers. Some of them tilled the soil, but most of them were just wandering herdsmen. Then, in the twelfth century before Christ, a new people arrived. They were called the Phoenicians. They came from Asia Minor, and they established a number of trading-stations along the coast.

For several hundred years the Phoenicians were content with these small settlements. They used them to provision their ships while they were trading in the western Mediterranean. But in 814 B.C. they founded the city of Carthage. It was built on a small peninsula about 10 miles (16 kilometres) from the centre of present-day Tunis.

The city of Carthage gradually rose to considerable import-ance. Inland from it stretched some of the richest farming land in the world; and there were iron and lead mines near by. In addition, the local people were already skilled in pottery-making and carpet-weaving. This provided the Carthaginians

As in the days of Carthage, the people of North Africa are skilled potters. Here, some of their work is set out for sale in a Moroccan market

North Africa has a long tradition of carpet-weaving. Our picture shows a carpet-seller and his wares

with valuable merchandise to sell in other Mediterranean lands.

By 400 B.C. the Carthaginians controlled the whole of the North African coastline almost as far east as Egypt. They also ruled Sicily, Sardinia and the southern half of Spain. But, unlike many other conquerors, the Carthaginians were not a fierce warlike people. Their aim was always to live peaceably among their new neighbours, and grow rich on trade.

It was, in fact, the enormous wealth of the Carthaginians that finally led to their downfall. It made the Romans so envious of them that the Romans made up their minds to conquer the "Punici", as they called them. (In Latin the word "Punicus" means "Phoenician". We still sometimes use the

17

adjective "Punic" when we are referring to something which is connected with Carthage.)

There were three long drawn out wars between Rome and Carthage. In the second, which lasted for sixteen years, the Carthaginians were led by their famous general, Hannibal. Hannibal crossed the Alps with a fighting force that included one hundred elephants. He meant to attack Rome, but his men were driven back by the highly trained Roman soldiers.

By the time the second war was over the Carthaginians had lost nearly the whole of their empire. Then, at the end of the third war, in 146 B.C., the Romans burned Carthage itself to the ground. From then on, the former Carthaginian territory

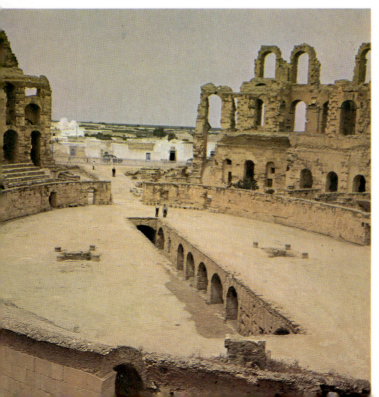

**The Romans built many fine buildings in North Africa. These are the remains of the Coliseum at El Djem, Tunisia**

was known as the Roman Province of Africa. (It was not until several centuries later that the name "Africa" came to be applied to the whole continent.)

About one hundred years after the Romans defeated the Carthaginians, they also conquered the Egyptians. For nearly five centuries the whole of North Africa was part of the great Roman Empire. The North Africans did not like being ruled by the Romans. But the Romans gave the region many fine cities. They also constructed roads to link these cities, and built aqueducts to bring water down to them from the hills.

When the Romans left, the Vandals, a war-like people from Germany, conquered the western part of North Africa. They stayed in Africa for nearly a century, but made little lasting impression on the country. Then, in the seventh century after Christ, the whole of North Africa was overrun by wave after wave of new invaders. They came from the lands east of the Red Sea, and were known as Arabs.

## Later Days

In ancient times, Arabs were only found in the Arabian Peninsula. Some of them lived a settled life in small towns or villages, but most of them were wandering herdsmen. These early Arabs were not aware that they were one nation. The only loyalty they felt was towards their tribe, and a great deal of inter-tribal fighting went on.

It was not until the middle of the seventh century after Christ that the Arabs suddenly felt a sense of brotherhood. The man who brought about this dramatic change was the great prophet, Mohammed. He not only gave the Arabs a new religion—Islam—but also a common purpose. This purpose was nothing less than to conquer the entire world, in order to spread the new faith.

The Arabs set about this task with a fanatical zeal. Less than one hundred years after the death of Mohammed, their territory extended right from the shores of the Atlantic Ocean to the borders of China. It was an even larger empire than the Romans had ruled at the height of their power. And, wherever the Arabs went, they forced people, at the point of the sword, to accept Islam.

Among the lands which the Arabs conquered was the whole of North Africa. The Egyptians, who were attacked first, offered little resistance, and their country was overrun in about A.D. 640. The rest of North Africa, which was mainly inhabited by the Berbers, fought tooth and nail against the invaders; but, by A.D. 700, even the fiercest of the North Africans had been subdued, and were (outwardly, at least) followers of Mohammed.

It was quite clear, however, that the Berbers deeply resented their foreign rulers. They constantly rebelled against the Arab governors, and there was a great deal of bloodshed and misery.

20

Throughout North Africa there is ample evidence of the spread of Islam. This *marabout* (the tomb of a local Moslem holy man) is one of many to be found in the region

Finally, in about A.D. 800, the Arab leader Caliph Harun-al-Rashid (the same caliph who appears in *A Thousand and One Nights*) gave up his claim to the whole of North Africa, except Egypt.

As a result, many of the Arabs fled hastily back to Arabia; but this did not mean that Arab influence was at an end in North Africa. Although the Berbers had hated the Arabs ruling their country, many of them had adopted the Arab way of life. There had also been a considerable amount of inter-marriage between the two peoples over the years.

21

The five or six centuries that followed were the "Golden Age" in the history of North Africa. Never before or since have the North Africans enjoyed such a continuous period of peace and prosperity. This was partly the result of the conquests the North Africans made in Sicily and Spain; but it was due even more to the position they held as the "middle-men" or "go-betweens" for a large part of the world's trade.

The North Africans had been taught to be traders by their Arab rulers. They knew that if they travelled south, beyond the Sahara, or east, beyond the Red Sea, they could obtain many things for which people in European countries would pay very highly. In particular, they brought back spices, silks, perfumes, precious stones and ivory. All these they carried across the Mediterranean, and sold at a huge profit in Spain, Italy or France.

It was during this long period of prosperity that Arab scholarship was at its height in North Africa. Learned men studied the classical Greek writings, and carefully translated them into their own language. To the knowledge they obtained from the Greeks they added the ideas they had acquired from their contact with the eastern countries. Later, most of this learning was passed on to the Europeans, and it played a considerable part in bringing about the Renaissance.

The decline of the "Golden Age" in North Africa began in about the fifteenth century after Christ. By this time, the European countries were rapidly emerging from the Middle Ages, and were becoming rich and powerful. Soon the

Europeans were no longer willing to employ the North Africans as "middle-men" when they wanted to import goods. Instead, they began seeking out their own trade routes to the Spice Islands and the East.

In a few short years the North Africans found they had lost nearly all their wealth and importance. This was bad enough; but while they were still trying to recover, an even greater disaster befell them. The Turks, who had already conquered all the lands around the eastern end of the Mediterranean, decided to add North Africa to their empire. By the end of the sixteenth century they had overrun the whole of the region, except Morocco.

The North Africans naturally hated losing their independence once again; but, as time went on, they gradually became more and more friendly with the Turks.

One reason for this was that the Turks shared the same religious faith as the North Africans. In fact, the Turkish sultan even claimed to be a direct descendant of Mohammed.

Another, equally important, reason was that the Turks did not object to the Barbary pirates. These were ruthless North African sea-rovers, who attacked and robbed any Christian merchant vessels they could find. During the seventeenth century, Algiers, Tripoli and Tunis all lived luxuriously on their pirate booty. Even Salé, a city in independent Morocco, grew enormously rich as the result of its piracy.

At first, the Europeans tried by bribery to persuade the North African countries to leave their merchant shipping alone. When this failed, they decided that they would have to wipe out the Barbary pirates by force. They did this so successfully that by the beginning of the nineteenth century many of the former pirate strongholds were almost in ruin; but what finally put an end to the pirate raids was the desire of the European countries for colonial expansion.

It was the French who first succeeded in colonizing part of North Africa. After suffering crushing defeats in the Napoleonic Wars, they were determined to prove that they were a great power once again. In 1830 they captured Algiers and most of the coastal area around it. Then, in 1881, they marched into Tunisia, under the pretext of saving it from an invasion by the Italians.

By this time, Great Britain had considerable financial interests in Egypt. The British Government had, in particular, supplied much of the money needed for the construction of the Suez Canal. Not unnaturally, the British people were anxious that their investments should be safe. So, when there were internal disturbances in Egypt in 1882, Britain decided to occupy the country.

Now only the area between Egypt and Tunisia remained under Turkish control. This was eventually conquered by the Italians, in 1912, and united to form the new country of Libya.

It was also in 1912 that Morocco, which had remained independent for so long, was finally conquered. Most of Morocco became French but the rest became Spanish, as both nations claimed they had a right to the country.

## Islam

Mohammed, the founder of the religion called Islam, was born in about A.D. 570. He was born and brought up in Mecca, a town in the Arabian Peninsula.

At the time of Mohammed's birth, the Arabs were still a pagan people. They worshipped the sun, moon and stars, and countless unseen spirits they called djinns.

As Mohammed grew older, he became dissatisfied with this primitive religion. It seemed to him that the Christians and Jews were right when they said that there was only one God. Then, one night, he had a vision in which an angel spoke to him. The angel said that there was only one true God, Allah, and that he had chosen Mohammed to be his Prophet.

A typical mosque—note the modern touch: a loudspeaker in the minaret which is used to call the people to prayer

Mohammed was deeply moved by this divine revelation. He began urging everyone to give up the old pagan beliefs, and to believe in the one all-powerful Creator. But most of the people of Mecca thought that Mohammed was either a liar or a madman. After several years of teaching and preaching, he had still made only a handful of converts there.

Mohammed grew so despondent that in A.D. 622 he decided to leave Mecca and go to Medina. This was a town about 250 miles (400 kilometres) to the north, where he already had a number of followers. To his delight, the people of Medina received him with great enthusiasm. They were so impressed by his teaching that they even asked him to become the ruler of their city.

Mohammed then decided to spread his new religion by force of arms. He told his followers that every drop of blood they shed was equivalent to two months spent in prayer. Finally, in A.D. 630, Mohammed returned to Mecca as a conqueror. In a very short time he was the spiritual leader of the entire Arab world.

Mohammed, unlike Christ, never claimed that he was God, and his followers do not worship him. For this reason, the followers of Mohammed do not like it when people call them Mohammedans. The correct name for them is Moslems, which means "people who submit to God's will". Similarly, the correct name for the religion which Mohammed founded is Islam, which means "submission to God".

Utter submission is the key-note of the religion of Islam.

Whatever happens to them, good or bad, the Moslems always accept it as being the will of Allah. It is sometimes said that this is the reason why the Arabs are so slow to improve their way of life. They feel that it is useless to make plans when it is Allah who will decide the course of events.

The Moslem equivalent to the Bible is the Koran. It is a collection of the sayings of Mohammed, which Moslems believe were inspired directly by God. The sayings were collected together by some of Mohammed's friends about a year after his death in A.D. 632. They give the Moslems instructions which cover almost every aspect of their lives.

Islam differs from most religions in having no specially trained ministers. The *khatib* (who preaches to the people) and the *imam* (who leads the prayers) are just ordinary Moslems. They are chosen for their piety and learning, but they are not granted any particular privileges. Most of them spend only a few hours a week on their religious duties, and do some other kind of work the rest of the time.

Moslem places of worship are known as mosques. They usually have a dome, and a slender tower called a minaret, with a crescent on top. In Morocco, Tunisia and Libya non-Moslems are strictly forbidden to enter the mosques; but in Egypt and in certain parts of Algeria they are nearly always admitted.

Before entering a mosque, both Moslems and non-Moslems must take off their shoes or cover them with canvas slippers. This is done partly out of reverence, and partly to keep the dust

27

The outer courtyard of a Tunisian mosque. Note the shoes which the worshippers have left outside when they entered the mosque itself

from the streets out of the mosques. Moslems are also expected to wash their face, hands and feet before they enter. In the courtyard of every mosque there is a fountain, or a tank of clean water, where this can be done.

To Christians, the interior of a mosque often seems empty and uninteresting. Usually, the only furniture is an elaborately carved pulpit with steps leading up from the front. There are no seats or benches. Each Moslem kneels on a small mat or rug, and touches the ground with his forehead over and over again as he prays.

Christians also notice the absence of pictures and statues.

28

These are never seen in a mosque, or anywhere else in the Arab world, for that matter. Moslems believe that it is wrong to try to copy living things. This is the reason why all Arabic decoration consists of geometrical designs, or is based on Arabic writing.

To the Moslems the most important feature of a mosque is the *mihrab*. This is a tall, arched recess in one of the walls, usually close to the pulpit. When the Moslems pray they always look towards the *mihrab*, and then they know they are looking towards Mecca. It is one of the commandments of their religion that they must face the Prophet's birth-place when they pray.

The Moslems' holy day, equivalent to the Christian Sunday, is Friday. Most of the shops and businesses close on a Friday, so that the men can go to the mosques. In some places, women also attend but they are not allowed to join in the public wor-

A view of the inside of the beautiful mosque of Moulay Ismail in Meknes, Morocco. Above the two pillars are splendid examples of the decorative use of Arabic script

ship. They sit either in a balcony or in a special area partitioned off from the main part of the mosque.

Every day of the week Moslems are supposed to face Mecca and pray five times—at dawn, at midday, in the afternoon, at sunset and after dark. They sometimes go to the mosque to say these prayers; but it is not uncommon to see them unrolling their prayer-mats at home, at work or even by the side of the road.

When it is time for prayer, an official called a *muezzin* cries in a loud voice: "*Allahu akbar, la ilaha illa Allah!*" ("Allah is great and there is no god but Allah!") At one time the *muezzin* used to climb onto a small balcony at the top of the minaret to call the faithful; but nowadays the voice of the *muezzin* is often recorded, and is just relayed from the minaret.

One month in the year is known to Moslems as Ramadan. It is a time, rather like Lent, when they try to purify their lives and grow closer to God. During Ramadan, Moslems may neither eat nor drink while it is daylight. Officially, daylight begins as soon as it is possible to tell a white thread from a black one, and ends when the two threads can no longer be told apart.

As the Moslem calendar is a lunar calendar, Ramadan falls eleven days later each year. It is exacting even when it falls in the winter; but it must require tremendous devotion and self-denial to go without the least sip of water the whole of a long, scorching day in summer. Nevertheless, all strict Moslems, both men and women, observe the fast faithfully. When it is

30

over everyone celebrates with three days of feasting and jollity.

To Moslems, the most important date in history is the day Mohammed left Mecca for Medina. They call this the *Hegira*, which is Arabic for "flight" or "departure". According to our calendar, this took place on July 16th, 622; but to the Moslems it was the first day of the year 1, as it marked the beginning of the new Moslem Era.

## *Daily Life*

Roughly one quarter of the people of North Africa are city-dwellers. Most of them live in five- or six-storey blocks of flats, with balconies where they can sit in warm weather. If they are

**A view of modern Rabat. In cities such as this most people are flat-dwellers**

poor, they usually live in the centre of the city; but if they are better off they often live in the suburbs and travel to work by bus or train every day.

Many shops and offices open at seven or eight o'clock in the morning. To make up for this early start, there is a long lunch-hour, from noon to three or four o'clock in the afternoon. During the lunch-hour, everyone goes home for the main meal of the day. There is usually also time for a short rest before returning to work.

The midday meal is often some form of *cous-cous*. This is the staple dish in all the North African countries, with the exception of Egypt. It is made by steaming semolina over a saucepan of boiling vegetables. When the semolina is cooked, it is mixed with small pieces of vegetables, meat, chicken or sometimes fish.

In Egypt the staple food is not semolina but rice. A plate of

**A street in the old city of Tetuan. Note the bread on sale to the right of the picture**

rice is always served at the main meal of the day, often with small pieces of lamb.

Bread is eaten at all meals in the North African countries. The loaves are generally pancake-shaped, and roughly the size of a dinner plate.

When work is over, the North Africans like to spend the evening with friends. They listen to the radio, or watch television programmes, which can be received in most North African cities. They sip Turkish coffee, or their favourite drink —mint tea. They never drink any wine or spirits, however, as this is forbidden by the Moslem religion.

Many of the men who work in the cities of North Africa like to wear European clothes. Others still prefer the traditional *djellaba*, a long, loose gown with a hood. Over the *djellaba* they sometimes wear a hooded cloak called a *burnous*. On their heads they may wear either a turban, or a maroon-coloured pill-box hat called a fez.

Even a man who wears European clothes often insists that his wife and daughters wear native dress. This generally consists of a long, black or white robe, which covers the whole body from head to foot. In most parts of North Africa women also wear a veil. This may be either part of the head-dress drawn across the face, or a separate, small piece of material, called a yashmak.

In all the North African countries women are regarded as inferior to men. This idea is often blamed on Mohammed, but it was an accepted Arab belief long before the days of Islam.

Veiled women in the *souk* of the Tetuan *medina*

In fact, Mohammed made some effort to improve the position of Moslem women. For instance, he forbade a man to marry more than four wives, as many Arab men had done in the past.

Very few women in the cities go out to work. This is partly due to tradition, and partly to lack of education and training. The average Moslem woman will not even enter a café or restaurant. Often, the only time she leaves the house is to go to the market or *souk*, to do her shopping.

The *souk* is nearly always in the oldest quarter of the city. This means that the shops are in narrow, twisting alleys, which are sometimes covered with rush-matting to keep out the sun. The shops themselves are usually little more than large, open-fronted cupboards. In some of them the craftsmen squat on the ground busily making the goods they then display for sale.

In most parts of North Africa going shopping means having to bargain. The shopkeeper asks a price for his goods, the customer offers him a much smaller amount, and this continues until eventually they come to an agreement. Neither the shopkeeper nor the customer is trying to cheat the other. It is just that the North Africans regard bargaining as an enjoyable part of buying and selling!

Life in the villages in North Africa is very different from life in the big cities. Most of the villagers work on the land, and they are often out in the fields from early morning until dusk. Sometimes the women help their menfolk, especially at harvest time. Even the children give a hand, looking after the sheep and goats, and doing other simple jobs.

The wives or children take the midday meal to the farmworkers in the fields. When the men have eaten it, they usually go to sleep for an hour or two under a tree or in a ditch.

The main meal of the day is the evening meal which all the family eat together at home. It consists of either semolina or rice, and vegetables, bread and fruit. Meat of any kind is a luxury.

Most villagers live in a house made of adobe—sun-dried bricks. The family sit on the floor, on rugs or matting, to eat their meals or talk to guests. They also sleep on the floor, on mattresses which are rolled up during the day. Cooking is done either on a primus stove, or over a crude fireplace, which may be either inside or outside the house.

Village people nearly always wear traditional dress. Sometimes the women hold their garments in place with a sash at the waist, which also serves as a pouch for carrying small possessions. Country women like to dye their hands and feet with henna. They also love jewellery. Often their bracelets, necklaces and ear-rings are the only articles of any real value which they possess.

Unfortunately, disease is rife in nearly all the agricultural areas of North Africa. One of the most widespread complaints is an infection of the eyes, called trachoma, which is carried by flies. Another common disease, which robs the sufferer of all his energy, is called bilharzia. It is caused by a parasite which lives in marshy water, and is particularly common in the villages on the banks of the Nile.

Wherever the North Africans live, in town or country, they are a very courteous people. When two friends meet in the street, they always shake hands and say, *"As-salaam alaykum!"* ("Peace be upon you!"). The reply to this is: *"Wa-alaykum as-salaam!"* ("Peace be upon you, too!"). They then both exchange many flowery compliments before mentioning any really important matter they may wish to discuss.

North African people also have a very strong sense of family responsibility. They consider it their duty to give help to any relative who may be in need, even if he is only a distant cousin. Older members of the family are always cared for as a matter of course. They live with their children and grandchildren, and are treated by everyone with the greatest respect and affection.

# Schools and Colleges

One of the most familiar sounds in North Africa is a high-pitched chanting. It tells everyone within earshot that children are attending an old Koranic school near by. Each of these schools belongs to a mosque, but the two are not always together. The school may be quite a distance away, in a private house, a hut or a room behind a shop.

The children who attend these schools are all boys, aged between five and twelve. They squat cross-legged in a circle round their teacher, who holds a long stick in one hand. The boys have no books, but they usually balance a small board on their knees. They write on these boards with a reed pen dipped in a thin ink made from burnt wool and water.

The method of teaching is practically always the same. The teacher reads a verse from the Koran, and the boys repeat it over and over again, swaying backwards and forwards as they do so. Then the boys write down on their boards the verses they have been repeating. Any boy who has not learnt all the verses by heart by the end of the day is likely to get a beating.

Occasionally, a little reading and writing and some simple arithmetic are also taught at the Koranic schools. How much the boys learn, however, depends chiefly on how much the teacher himself happens to know! The boys usually go to school for a few hours every day, except Friday. On the last day

37

of the week, Thursday, they give the teacher a small payment, either in money or in kind.

For centuries the Koranic schools have been the only places in North Africa where children could receive any education. As a result, the vast majority of the people have remained more or less illiterate. Even when the European colonists arrived there was little improvement. The colonists built schools for their own children, but did practically nothing for the children of the native population.

It was only with the coming of independence that the situation began to change. Before long, each of the North African countries had accepted in principle the idea of free, compulsory schooling for all children. Just how soon this will be achieved depends on the amount of money available. At present, it is chiefly in the large towns that the old Koranic schools have been replaced by modern primary and secondary schools.

The new state schools are being run on much the same lines as schools in Europe. The aim is that the children should spend twelve years at school, and then take an examination before leaving. At the moment, however, the lack of teachers is a great problem. Sometimes there are over one hundred children in a class; and sometimes the children can only attend school in shifts.

Both boys and girls are admitted to the new state schools. In most places, however, the boys easily outnumber the girls, as there is still considerable prejudice against girls being educated. All the children wear European clothes when they go to school,

**This school classroom—in Libya—is very different from that of the traditional Koranic school. The writing on the blackboard is Arabic and must be read from right to left**

and carry large satchels under their arms. The younger children also wear long-sleeved black pinafores, as the children do in France.

The universities, like the schools, were at one time closely connected with the mosques. They taught little except Koranic studies, Moslem law, and sometimes mathematics and logic. They chiefly provided a place where saintly men could lead lives of religious contemplation. They also ensured that the Moslem faith was handed down from one generation to the next exactly as Mohammed had taught it.

39

The most famous of these old universities is the Karaouine at Fez, in Morocco. It was founded in the ninth century after Christ, several hundred years before Oxford or Cambridge. For more than one thousand years Moslem scholars have been coming to the Karaouine from all over the Arab world. Even today it still trains many of North Africa's future leaders and administrators.

About 1,600 students, all young men aged between thirteen and thirty, attend the Karaouine. Each student lives in a small, dark cell in a building called a *medersa*. These buildings are among the finest examples of Arabic architecture and art to be found anywhere; but they are also cold and insanitary, and it is not uncommon for the students to contract serious illnesses.

At the Karaouine, there are no lecture-rooms such as are found in European universities. The students sit cross-legged on small mats in the courtyard of the mosque. The teaching methods are similar to those used in Europe in the Middle Ages. The professor reads aloud from a book, and the students take notes which they have to learn by heart.

Another ancient seat of learning is the Al-Azhar University in Cairo. It was founded in A.D. 972, and is known as the "Mother University" of the Moslem world. It has 20,000 students, some of them from distant parts of Africa and Asia. They receive their education entirely free, and if they are poor they are also provided with food and money.

Like the schools, the universities have undergone many changes since the North African countries became independent. The older foundations have had modern departments added, and several new universities have been opened. In both of these the education is roughly the same as in Europe. There are faculties in all the usual subjects, and degrees are awarded after three to six years.

An important step has recently been taken in the universities. It has been decided to conduct many of the lectures in either English or French. This means that the students can now use up-to-date textbooks which are not available in Arabic. There has been some opposition to the change, as Arabic is regarded as a holy language, being the language of the Koran; but the change is now generally accepted as being essential, particularly for the study of medicine and science.

Another step forward has been the admission of women to places of higher education. In the Egyptian universities, for example, there is now on average one woman student to every four men. As a result, women are at last able to follow professional careers, if they wish. Already, there is a growing number of women in medicine, law, teaching and commerce.

When all the schools and universities were attached to the mosques there was little opportunity for sport. Nowadays, however, games form an important part of the curriculum in all state-run schools and colleges. The most popular games are soccer, tennis, basket-ball, volley-ball and swimming. Students who are outstanding at athletics sometimes compete in the Pan-Arab Olympic Games.

# Morocco

The name "Morocco" is a European corruption of "Marrakesh", the name of the largest and most important city in the south of the country. The Arabs themselves call Morocco "*Al Maghreb al-Aksa*", which means "The Land of the Furthest West". As you can see from a map, more than half of Morocco lies further west than Land's End.

Morocco is the smallest but one of the North African countries. Even so, it covers an area of roughly 170,000 square miles (440,000 square kilometres), or nearly six times that of Scotland. At the last census it had a population of about $15\frac{1}{2}$ million, but this is increasing very rapidly. Rather more than half the Moroccans are Arabs, and the rest are Berbers or people of Arab-Berber descent.

In the past, there were often outbreaks of violence between the Arabs and the Berbers in Morocco. During one of these disturbances, in 1912, the French decided to take over the country. For the next forty-six years, ninety per cent of Morocco was a French Protectorate. Only the city of Tangier and a small area bordering on the Mediterranean Sea were not under the control of the French.

The French undoubtedly did a great deal to develop the resources of Morocco. For example, they increased the country's wheat production ten times, the number of its date palms five times and of its olive trees forty times. They established factories and sank phosphate mines, and laid a complete net-

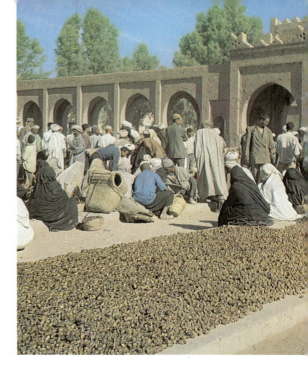

The date crop increased enormously under the French administration in Morocco. These dates displayed for sale in an oasis market are a typical Moroccan sight

work of railway lines. They also opened nearly five hundred hospitals; there was only one in the whole of the country in 1912.

Nevertheless, the Moroccans became more and more resentful of the French. One reason for this was that the French owned practically all the land which could be profitably cultivated. Another was that the French held virtually every post in the country's administration. Added to this, the Moroccans knew that the French secretly had no respect for them and regarded them as ignorant peasants.

For a time, the Moroccans did little or nothing about their grievances. Then, during the Second World War, they saw the country that was "protecting" them overrun by the Germans.

43

After this, the Moroccans began clamouring for their freedom. By the early 1950s, there were constant displays of violence, resulting in a great deal of bloodshed and bitterness.

Finally, in March, 1956, the French gave up all claims to Morocco. In April of the same year, the Spaniards also gave up their claims to the small area they ruled in the north of the country. Then the various Western powers who controlled Tangier decided that it was time for them to withdraw. When this happened, the whole of the ancient kingdom of Morocco became an independent nation once again.

The present ruler of Morocco is King Hassan II. He came to the throne on the sudden death of his father in February, 1961. He is interested in politics, and takes an active part in the government of the country. In fact, he is said to work harder and longer than almost anyone else in Morocco!

**Dancers of the High Atlas region**

A Chaouen street scene.
This mountain city in
the Rif was once
considered holy

Well over one third of Morocco is mountainous. In the north
are the Rif Mountains, and further south the Middle Atlas, the
High Atlas and the Anti Atlas. All these ranges, except the Rif,
run roughly south-west to north-east across the country. In the
east, the Middle Atlas and the High Atlas merge to form a
barren tableland.

The Rif Mountains stretch in a gentle curve from Chaouen
to the Algerian border. The highest point is Mount Tidiguin,
which rises to more than 8,000 feet (2,440 metres). Few visitors
are ever seen in the Rif, because of the lack of good roads; yet

45

the lower slopes are covered with vineyards and cedar forests, and are very attractive indeed.

The only people who live in the Rif Mountains are the Berbers. They can sometimes be seen in Tetuan or even in Tangier, buying and selling goods in the markets there. The women can easily be distinguished by their striped dresses, their head-shawls and their enormous straw hats. They are also noticeable because they are the only women in traditional dress who do not wear a veil.

The Middle Atlas range is well wooded and has numerous little rivers and lakes. People go there in the summer to shoot and fish, and in the winter to ski and toboggan in the snow. The High Atlas and the Anti Atlas, on the other hand, are mainly bare and forbidding. Apart from a few small Berber villages on the lower slopes, they are almost entirely deserted.

In the foothills of the Middle Atlas is the vast mining centre of Khouribga. In this area are some of the richest and most extensive deposits of phosphates in the world. Altogether, Morocco produces nearly twenty per cent of the world's total extraction of phosphates, and production is still increasing steadily.

Between the Atlas Mountains and the Atlantic Ocean is the most fertile region of Morocco. The chief produce is fruit of various kinds, particularly olives, almonds, oranges and figs. Cereals (mainly barley and wheat) are also grown on a considerable scale. In addition, there are large forests of cedar, cork-oak, eucalyptus and pine.

**Locally produced oranges, and other fruit and vegetables, on sale in Tangier**

South of the High Atlas the land quickly becomes semi-desert. The only vegetation is an occasional grove of palm-trees, growing in a dried-up river bed. Despite this, it is the most colourful and spectacular region in the whole of Morocco. In places the soil is crimson, and the rocks vary from sandstone red to green, yellow and silvery white.

It is in this region that most of Morocco's famous *kasbahs* are found. (A *kasbah* is a kind of fortified stronghold, rather similar to a medieval castle.) Some of the *kasbahs* are now deserted, and crumbling into ruin. In others, however, the people are still living much as their ancestors have been doing for centuries. The chief lives with his family in one of the square towers of the *kasbah*, and allows the peasants to scrape a living from his land. In return, they provide him with all his requirements. The

47

peasants themselves live in small mud huts, either inside or outside the high walls. There are usually about one hundred peasants living together in a *kasbah*.

The capital of Morocco is the city of Rabat. It stands at the mouth of the River Bou Regreg, and has approximately 400,000 inhabitants.

Like most cities in Morocco, Rabat is divided into two distinct districts. One is the old Arab quarter, called the *medina*, and the other is the modern European town. The *medina* of Rabat was originally built in the middle of the twelfth century. Much of this old town still exists, surrounded by its enormous, copper-coloured mud walls. The modern part of the town was laid out by the French. It has splendid, tree-lined avenues, with elegant buildings and a number of delightful public gardens.

The King of Morocco has his official home in the modern sector of the city. Every Friday when he is in residence he can be seen going in solemn procession from his palace to the nearby royal mosque. Dressed entirely in white, he is driven there in a gilded coach. On his return, he rides a white horse, and has a scarlet parasol held high over his head by a Negro guard.

Rabat is one of Morocco's four imperial cities, as they are called. Each has, at some time, been the official residence of the sultan or king.

The oldest of the four imperial cities is Fez. It was founded by King Moulay Idris II, a direct descendant of Mohammed, in the year A.D. 808.

Fez is often said to be the most oriental of the North African cities. Its *medina* is a maze of narrow, twisting alleys which seem

**A street in the *medina* of Fez**

dark even in the middle of the day. The *souk* in Fez is one of the largest and busiest in Morocco. It sells everything from rugs, pottery and copperwork to articles made from the world-famous Moroccan leather.

Only a short distance from Fez is the imperial city of Meknes. It was mainly built towards the end of the seventeenth century, on the orders of a king called Moulay Ismail. The show-piece of Meknes is the exquisite Bab el Mansour Gate. From a distance, it looks as if it is covered with blue and green tapestry, but it is in fact decorated entirely with tiles.

Rabat, Fez and Meknes are all in the region known as "white" Morocco. It is called this because most of the houses in

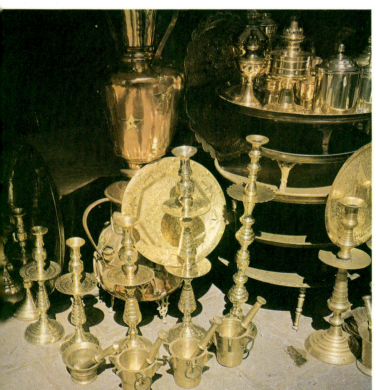

**Moroccan brass and copperware on sale in a local market**

the native quarters are made of mud and then whitewashed. The last of the four imperial cities, Marrakesh, is in "red" Morocco. In this region the houses are made of reddish-brown clay, which is left its natural colour.

Marrakesh is sometimes called "The Pearl of the South". Although it is almost on the edge of the Sahara, it has some of the loveliest surroundings in the whole of North Africa. On one side it is encircled by the snow-capped peaks of the High Atlas. On the other, there is a palm grove of more than 150,000 trees stretching far away into the distance.

The great *souk* at Marrakesh is always teeming with noisy, colourful life. It is the meeting-place for traders from every corner of Morocco and beyond. But even more exciting than the *souk* itself is the immense open space just outside it. This is the famous "Djemma el Fna", or "Place of the Dead". The best time to visit the Djemma el Fna is at dusk, when the kerosene lamps have just been lit. By this time most of the stall-holders have packed up, and the entertainers are taking their place. There are jugglers and acrobats, snake-charmers and fire-eaters, and, perhaps most fascinating of all, there are story-tellers who keep their circle of listeners absolutely enthralled.

The "summer capital" of Morocco is the city of Tangier. For two months every year the government moves there to escape the worst of the heat in Rabat.

Tangier has always been of importance because of its position at the entrance to the Mediterranean. In the Middle Ages it was captured first by the Portuguese, then by the

The Djemma el Fna in Marrakesh, where evening entertainment takes place every day. There are acrobats, jugglers, dancers, musicians and story-tellers

Spaniards and then by the Portuguese once again. In 1672 it came into the possession of Great Britain in a rather curious way. It formed part of the dowry of Catherine of Braganza when she married King Charles II. Samuel Pepys, the diarist, was at one time the Governor of Tangier. In fact, he supervised the evacuation of the British garrison in 1686 after the city was besieged by the Moroccans.

In 1923 Tangier became what was called an "international

city". It was under the control of a council of delegates from ten different countries, including Great Britain. Its imports and exports were all untaxed, and there were no restrictions on the exchange of currency. This made it a notorious centre for smugglers of all nationalities.

Today Tangier is both a free port and a popular international holiday resort. It is a lively city, with many first-class hotels and a long, sandy beach. Tangier also has one of the best climates

A story-teller in the Djemma el Fna. In a country where there are still many people who cannot read or write the story-teller is a familiar and popular figure

on the North African coast. Frost and ice are unknown, yet
even in the height of summer the temperature rarely exceeds
80° Fahrenheit (26° Centigrade).

None of the cities mentioned so far, except Rabat, has more
than a quarter of a million inhabitants. Casablanca, on the
other hand, has a population that is rapidly approaching one
million and a half. It stands on the Atlantic coast 56 miles (90
kilometres) south of Rabat, and is the industrial and commer-
cial centre of Morocco as well as its largest and busiest port.

At the end of the nineteenth century Casablanca was still
only a small fishing town. Today it seems more like a modern
city in the United States than a city in Morocco. It is not,

54

however, an attractive or well-planned city. It also has some of the worst slums in North Africa, where countless people live in the most appalling conditions.

**The courtyard of a Moroccan palace**

# Algeria

Algeria is easily the largest of the North African countries. It covers an area of approximately 1,100,000 square miles (2,850,000 square kilometres). This is nearly four times the area of France, but barely one-eighth of this vast country is fertile enough to be habitable. The rest of Algeria is nothing but an inhospitable expanse of trackless desert.

The fertile area of the country is the hilly region that borders the Mediterranean. Nowhere is it more than 220 miles (352 kilometres) in depth, and in some places it is considerably less. Practically all the people are crowded into this comparatively narrow strip. According to the latest figures, there are about eighteen million Algerians, but this population is increasing very rapidly.

Algeria was first united to form one country when it was conquered by the French. They landed near Algiers, in 1830, and quickly captured a large part of the coastal region. It took them nearly thirty years to gain possession of the rest of the country. In fact, the French formed their famous Foreign Legion to help them subdue the fierce Algerian tribesmen.

When the French came to Algeria it was a very backward, impoverished country. Most of the Algerians made their living by tilling the soil, but they had little or no knowledge of up-to-date farming methods. Under the French every patch of arable land was soon being intensely cultivated. The French also

56

A typical small town in Algeria, on the Trans-Saharan motor road

built a number of fine new towns, and linked them by means of good roads and railways.

The French never regarded Algeria as just a colony. They declared that the northern region was an integral part of France, merely divided from the rest of their country by the sea. In theory, this meant that the Algerians had the same rights as Frenchmen, and could send representatives to the French Assembly in Paris. Only the south of Algeria was a colony, and even this was officially governed from Algiers.

Despite this, the Algerians always felt bitter resentment of the French. They thought the French had stolen their country, and were merely developing it in order to benefit themselves.

57

There was undoubtedly a certain amount of truth in this accusation; after more than one hundred years of French rule, most native Algerians were still pitifully ignorant and poor.

Eventually, in November, 1954, armed rebellion broke out against the French. At first it seemed a small, unimportant affair; but before long it was clearly very serious. In the end, the fighting went on for over seven years. During that time, thousands of men, women and children were killed, and nearly two million people were made homeless.

The war only ended when France agreed to grant Algeria her freedom. Algeria is now an independent republic, ruled by a president and a house of representatives. The first Head of State was President Mohammed Ben Bella, who had been one of the leaders of the rebellion. He was elected in September, 1962. The present President of the Republic is Colonel Bendjedid Chadli, who took office in February, 1979.

One definite contribution that the French made to Algeria was the creation of the modern city of Algiers. When they arrived in 1830, Algiers was suffering from plague and famine, and was almost a ruin. Now it is a thriving capital with a population of approximately 1,500,000. As well as being the seat of Algeria's government, it is also one of the principal ports of North Africa.

The second largest city in Algeria is Oran, with a population of nearly half a million. It is also the largest seaport in the country, after Algiers. A great deal of wine, one of the country's most valuable exports, is shipped abroad from here. Unlike

**Vineyards near Tlemcen. Wine is one of Algeria's most valuable exports**

Algiers, Oran shows little signs of its long French occupation. Despite the fact that it is now expanding very rapidly, it still looks a typical, dusty old Arab town.

The third largest city in Algeria is Constantine. Although it is about 35 miles (56 kilometres) from the coast, it was an important trading-centre in the days of the Phoenicians. Its most striking feature is an immense gorge, which divides the city into two. The sides of the gorge are almost vertical and, at times, the River Rhumel (which runs at the bottom) becomes a torrent.

East of Algiers lies one of the most beautiful regions in North Africa. It consists of a range of low hills, called the Kabylia, which run parallel to the sea for about 125 miles (200 kilometres). Being hilly, the region has a very high rainfall, which produces lush vegetation. Even the tops of the hills are covered with magnificent forests of cork-oak and cedar.

The Kabylia is the home of a strange Berber people called the Kabyles. Although they are Moslems, they still retain their old pagan beliefs in magic and witchcraft. Most of the Kabyles live in small villages clinging to the sides of the hills. They make their living by keeping a few sheep and oxen, and growing figs, olives and corn.

Unfortunately, the Kabylia region is far too densely populated. In some places there are several hundred people trying to cultivate one square kilometre of land. Many of the Kabyles cannot even own a whole fig tree or olive tree. They have to be content with possessing a few branches of a tree that is shared by a number of families.

The only two motor-roads across the Sahara both start in Algeria. They both run north to south. (There are no roads at all across the Sahara from east to west.) The roads were constructed by the French between 1920 and 1930. Before that, the only way of crossing the desert was the same as it had been all down the ages—by camel.

Anyone wishing to drive along the desert motor-roads has to take a number of precautions. For instance, he must inform the appropriate officials well in advance that he intends to make the journey. These officials will radio to each of the villages he should pass through to say that he is coming. Then if he does not arrive at any of the villages on schedule a search-party will be sent out to look for him.

# *Tunisia*

Tunisia is by far the smallest of the five North African countries. It occupies a narrow strip of land bordered on two sides by the Mediterranean Sea. Tunisia is, however, the most fertile country in North Africa. The vast majority of its total population of 6,500,000 people are farmers.

For nearly three thousand years Tunisia was under the domination of foreign conquerors. The last of these were the French, who gained control of the country in 1881. Shortly before the Second World War a movement was begun to expel the French; but it was not until 1956 that Tunisia was finally declared an independent country.

**These women are washing sheepskins in the shallow water off the coast of Djerba. In the background is evidence of the foreign conquerors who once ruled the island—a Spanish fort**

The leader of the nationalists in their long struggle against the French was Habib Bourguiba. When Tunisia eventually won its freedom he was unanimously elected the country's first President. The "Great Champion", as President Bourguiba is called by the Tunisians, is still in office today. He rules the country with the help of a prime minister, a cabinet of other ministers and a house of elected representatives.

The political and economic centre of Tunisia is Tunis. It stands at the western end of a shallow lagoon, about six miles (nine kilometres) from the sea. In 1890 a channel was dug so that vessels up to twenty-foot (six-metre) draught could sail across the lagoon to Tunis. Larger vessels still have to dock at the outer port of La Goulette.

Tunis is one of the oldest cities on the Mediterranean coast. It helped Carthage in its wars against Rome and, after the destruction of Carthage, gave refuge to many of its inhabitants.

**A view of Tunis**

**The building which now houses the Tunisian National Assembly. It was built as a palace for the Bey or governor**

Today, Tunis has a population of nearly 550,000. The new town is typically European, but the old quarter is one of the most attractive Arab towns in North Africa.

In ancient times, the north of Tunisia was known as "the granary of the Roman Empire". It is still the chief grain-growing region of the country, although today little of the grain is exported. The only large town in this area, apart from Tunis, is Bizerta. During the French occupation of Tunisia, Bizerta was one of the most important naval bases in the Mediterranean.

South of the grain-growing area, Tunisia is divided into two distinct regions. To the west is the area known to the Arabs as the "Bled", and to the east is the "Sahel".

The Bled is mainly a monotonous, treeless plateau, where little or nothing will grow. In summer it is parched, while in winter it is windswept and bleak.

The only town in the Bled is the holy city of Kairouan. According to legend, when the Arab invaders first pitched their tents here, a spring of water miraculously appeared at their feet. Today, the Great Mosque at Kairouan is one of the most revered sanctuaries in the Moslem world. Kairouan is also known for the beautiful carpets which the native women have been making there for centuries.

The Sahel is a strip of low-lying fertile land, about thirty miles (forty-eight kilometres) wide. It stretches right down the eastern coast of Tunisia, roughly from Hammamet to the Island of Djerba.

Most of Tunisia's orchards and vineyards are found in the northern part of the Sahel. About half the produce is grown for home consumption, and the rest is exported.

The southern part of the Sahel is devoted chiefly to olive-growing. For long distances, there is nothing as far as the eye can see but the never-ending rows of olive trees. In one plantation alone there are more than eight million trees. This fantastic forest was laid out by the French in the early years of this century. In a good year, Tunisia can produce a vast quantity of olive-oil. Much of it is of a very high quality, and there is a

The *souk* in Sfax

great demand for it from overseas. Usually, about half the crop is exported—to every corner of the globe. This makes Tunisia the world's second largest exporter of olive-oil.

The most important town in the Sahel is Sfax. It is the second largest city in Tunisia, despite the fact that it has only about 170,000 inhabitants. The Arab quarter of Sfax is very ancient and picturesque. It is surrounded by a wall which was built more than one thousand years ago with stones from an old Roman city.

Sfax is one of the most important ports in Tunisia. Its deep harbour is used not only for exporting olive-oil, but also for shipping abroad an even more valuable commodity— phosphates. The phosphates are mainly found in the region around Gafsa, on the southern edge of the Bled. Like Morocco, Tunisia is one of the largest producers and exporters of phosphates in the world.

The Tunisian desert begins south of an imaginary line

65

joining Gafsa and Gabès. At first it is dotted with dozens of oases, varying in size from the largest in the whole of North Africa to quite small. The most important are Tozeur, which has 700,000 date palms, and Nefta with about 400,000 palms. About one tenth of the total date production of this area is exported each year.

About thirty miles (forty-eight kilometres) south of Gabès is one of the most curious villages in the world. It is called Matmata, and it stands on a bare plateau roughly 1,340 feet (409 metres) above sea-level.

At first glance all that can be seen at Matmata is a large number of huge, round pits. These pits are up to forty feet (twelve metres) in diameter and about thirty-three feet (ten metres) deep. They are, in fact, the people's underground homes. The entrance to each pit is a long, sloping tunnel, which runs from ground-level a little distance away. The floor of the pit forms a courtyard; and, in the walls of the pit, large holes are hollowed out to serve as rooms. All these underground homes have been dug out of the ground by hand, and some of them are very old. At the present time, Matmata has about 6,000 inhabitants, living in roughly 800 pit homes.

The troglodytes—or pit-dwellers—of Matmata still live almost exactly as their ancestors have been doing for centuries. The successive conquests which have changed the rest of North Africa so much seem to have left them completely unaffected. They rarely use a fire to cook their food, they know nothing of pottery, and have only the most elementary knowledge of spinning. What is more, they seem to have no desire at all to try to improve their way of life.

One of the most beautiful places in Tunisia is the Island of Djerba. According to classical mythology, it was here that the companions of Ulysses ate the fruit of the lotus tree, and completely forgot their homes and families in Greece.

The Island of Djerba has no springs or streams; it is watered entirely by wells. Apart from other vegetation, it has 500,000 olive trees and nearly 1,500,000 date palms. One of the principal trades on Djerba is the dangerous occupation of sponge-gathering. The fishermen, using stones to weigh themselves down, are dropped sixty or seventy feet (eighteen to twenty-one metres) over the side of a boat to gather the sponges from the sea-bed.

Today the "Lotus-Eaters' Island" is becoming popular as an international holiday resort. It has only a slight rainfall, a mild and even climate, and several beaches of very fine, white sand.

## Libya

Libya is a very unusual country for two reasons. The first is that Libya is one of the least inhabited territories in the world. It is the fourth largest country in Africa, with an area of nearly 700,000 square miles (1,800,000 square kilometres); yet its population is little more than 3,250,000.

**An oasis in the Fezzan province of Libya. The spring forms the centre of the whole oasis**

The second reason is that the land we now call Libya used to be three separate countries. They were Tripolitania and the Fezzan in the west, and Cyrenaica in the east. These three were only united in 1934, when they were all conquered by Italy. They then became known as the three provinces of the new country of Libya.

After the defeat of Italy in the Second World War, the United Nations Organisation was asked to decide Libya's future. Their decision was that it should be an independent state. In December 1959, Libya was declared a monarchy under King Idris I. But, less than ten years later, in September

1969, the king was deposed and the country became the Libyan Arab Republic.

Libya is now ruled by a committee called the Revolutionary Council. Its official aim is to make the new republic into a modern, forward-looking Arab nation. The Chairman of the Council is Colonel Muammar Al Gaddafi.

Although Libya is now officially one nation, the three provinces have very little contact with each other. This is easily understood by anyone looking at a map of the country. The inhabited part of Tripolitania is divided from the inhabited part of Cyrenaica by 400 miles (640 kilometres) of desert. Until a few years ago there was not even a road running between the two provinces. The Fezzan, which lies in the south, is still more inaccessible. It consists almost entirely of desert, with here and there a small village around an oasis. There are no roads, and very few landmarks to point the way. Until the introduction of air travel, the Fezzan was totally unknown to most of the Libyans themselves.

The capital of Libya, as well as its chief port, is Tripoli. It stands on a small peninsula, and looks particularly attractive when it is seen from the sea. Nearly a quarter of the country's entire population lives in or around Tripoli. This is the area where most of the newly developed industries are to be found.

Benghazi, the chief city and port of Cyrenaica, is Libya's second city. During the Second World War Benghazi changed hands five times before it was finally captured by the British. Nowadays, there is little to remind people of those dreadful

**A view of Tripoli**

times. Benghazi is rapidly becoming a pleasant modern city, with fine new buildings springing up everywhere.

The fertile coastal strip of Libya runs through both Tripolitania and Cyrenaica. With careful irrigation, it can be made to produce tomatoes, dates, potatoes, citrus fruits and various other crops. Further inland there is a broken chain of hills or, in Arabic, *djebels*. Most kinds of fruit and cereal will grow there, as the *djebels* have a fairly high winter rainfall.

At one time Libya's most valuable crop was esparto grass (or alfalfa). This is used to make high-quality paper such as that needed for the printing of bank-notes. For centuries, esparto grass has grown wild on the plains around Tripoli; but many of the former esparto areas are now desert, owing to the people's short-sighted farming methods.

70

Until a few years ago, esparto grass was practically the only export of Libya. There seemed to be nothing else the country could produce which could be sold overseas. Then, in 1959, a very exciting and far-reaching event took place. An American company discovered a vast quantity of oil beneath the Libyan desert.

Today, Libya is one of the leading oil-producing countries of the world. Nearly the whole of its vast crude-oil output is exported, chiefly to Europe.

The discovery of oil has already had a fairy-tale effect on the country's economy. From being one of the poorest nations in the world, the Libyans are now one of the richest. Roughly half the profits from the oil-wells are paid to the Libyan government as royalties. The government spends nearly three-quarters of

**Oil fires in the desert**

this money expanding the social services and developing the resources of the country.

One of the most striking changes has occurred in education. At the time when Libya became independent less than ten per cent of the children stayed at school long enough to learn to read and write. Now eighty-five per cent of all Libyan children attend primary school; many of them go on to secondary schools, and some continue their studies at one of Libya's two new universities.

There has also been a dramatic improvement in Libya's medical services. In 1959 there were only twenty-eight doctors in the whole country, but by 1966 there were no less than seven hundred. A start has also been made on providing a modern health service, available to everyone, free of charge. Already, fully-equipped mobile clinics are giving on-the-spot treatment to people living in the thinly populated desert regions.

The government realizes, of course, that the wealth from the oil-fields will come to an end eventually. It knows that Libya

A new mosque in Tripoli with a new office block facing it. Buildings like these are evidence of the country's new prosperity

**The remains of the Roman theatre at Leptis Magna**

is still basically an agricultural country, and it is spending large sums on making the land more productive. The government also believes that new industries will help to ensure permanent prosperity. A wide variety of goods is already being produced, ranging from cigarettes and sweets, to aluminium and cement.

Unfortunately, because of the unfavourable rate of exchange for most foreign currencies, not many tourists visit Libya. This is a pity since the beaches are good and the sea is warm enough for bathing most of the year. There must also be many people who would like to visit Libya's famous archaeological remains. The two best-known Romans sites are Leptis Magna and Sabratha, both within easy reach of Tripoli. They are among

74

the most interesting and extensive Roman ruins in the world. There are also the splendid Greek remains at Cyrene, the city which gave its name to Cyrenaica. It was built by Greek colonists about six hundred years before Christ.

# Egypt

Egypt lies the furthest east of all the North African countries.

It is roughly square in shape, and covers an area of approximately 386,000 square miles (1,000,000 square kilometres). This is nearly twice the size of France, or four times the size of Great Britain.

Although Egypt seems a large country, little more than three per cent of the land is fertile enough to be habitable. This means that a total population of more than 43,000,000 people live in an area of approximately 12,000 square miles (31,000 square kilometres).

The fertile part of the country is the strip of land that borders

**Fishing in the Nile**

the River Nile. In southern (or Upper) Egypt this strip is less than half a mile (one kilometre) wide, but later it broadens to 8–10 miles (12–16 kilometres). In northern (or Lower) Egypt the river fans out to form a delta. Here there is a large, triangular-shaped region of extremely fertile ground.

The modern history of Egypt began in the early nineteenth century. It was then that a remarkable man named Mohammed Ali first arrived in the country. He was the leader of a group of Albanians, who were engaged by the Turks (who then ruled Egypt) to help defend the country against Napoleon and his armies.

Mohammed Ali was quickly recognized as an outstanding

administrator. As a result, after the war was over, he was asked to stay in Egypt to help rebuild the ruined country. This was no easy task, as Egypt was little more than a devastated battlefield. But Mohammed Ali succeeded so well that the Turks later made him the ruler of Egypt, an honour and responsibility which his descendants were to inherit from him.

It was Mohammed Ali's grandson, the Khedive Ismail, who helped Egypt to take its next stride forward. He decided to have a canal dug to link the Mediterranean with the Red Sea. A glance at a map shows the enormous importance of such a canal. It meant that ships could sail directly to Europe from India and the East without having to make the long voyage round the Cape of Good Hope.

The Suez Canal, as it came to be called, was designed by a Frenchman named Ferdinand de Lesseps. It was begun in 1859, and completed, after a number of interruptions, ten years later. The Suez Canal runs for nearly 100 miles (160 kilometres) from Port Said in the north to the town of Suez in the south. It is at least 197 feet (60 metres) wide, and 34 feet (10 metres) deep for the whole of its length.

When the canal was finished, it was operated jointly by the British and the French. Britain also stationed a permanent garrison in the Canal Zone to protect it from possible attack. By the early 1880s, however, there was such unrest in Egypt that the garrison no longer seemed adequate. So, in 1882, Britain decided to take control of the whole country.

During the time of the British Protectorate, as it was called,

**Harvesting Egyptian cotton**

Britain did a great deal to develop Egypt's resources. In particular, a vast cotton industry was established in the fertile Nile Delta. As time went on, however, the Egyptians began accusing the British of exploiting the country. As a result, Britain withdrew most of her troops; and, in 1922, the Protectorate came to an end.

When the British left, Egypt became a kingdom once again, ruled by the descendants of Mohammed Ali. At first, all seemed well; but the Egyptians were soon making the same allegations against the king as they had made against the British. They particularly disliked the fact that a mere handful of wealthy people owned practically all the farming land, while the wage earned by the *fellahin* was barely enough to keep them alive.

By 1952, there was such strong opposition to the government that the king (King Farouk) was forced to abdicate. For a year his infant son was, in name, the Head of State. Then Egypt was declared an independent republic.

The present ruler of Egypt is President Muhammad Hosni Mubarak. He was confirmed as President by a public referendum in October, 1981, after the assassination of the previous head of state, President Sadat.

One of the first actions of the new government when Egypt became a republic was to confiscate all the large estates of the wealthy landowners. These were broken up into numerous small plots of ground, and given to the poor. Today, no individual in Egypt is allowed to own more than a specified area of land. This means that the ordinary agricultural worker has the opportunity to be his own master for the first time.

Since Egypt has become a republic the educational system

**The Aswan Dam**

of the country has been greatly extended. Several million more children are now attending school than in 1952. Many new factories have been opened, including a number of steel-works. There has also been a considerable improvement in the medical services.

The greatest single achievement since Egypt became a republic has been the construction of the Aswan High Dam. This is one of the most remarkable engineering feats of modern times. The dam holds back the water of the River Nile in Upper Egypt, and then releases it through huge sluices whenever it is required. This extends the season when crops can be grown in the Nile Valley. It is also increasing the area of land which can be cultivated.

The new High Dam has another very important aspect. It provides Egypt with an invaluable new source of power, which was seriously lacking in the past. Since the dam was built its hydro-electric plants have provided Egypt with six times as much electricity as was available before. This is extremely useful not only for domestic purposes, but also for supplying power to all the new factories which are being built.

The official name for Egypt today is the United Arab Republic. This was the title given jointly to both Egypt and Syria when they united in Fabruary, 1958. The Egyptians hoped that this would be the beginning of a federation of all the Arab nations; but, in fact, Syria withdrew from the union only three years later, and no other Arab states have so far applied to join.

The capital of Egypt is the city of Cairo. It was founded in A.D. 969, by a tribe of Moslem invaders called the Fatemites. Today, with a population of more than 5,000,000, it is not only the largest city in North Africa, but also the largest city in the entire Arab world.

The Mokattam Hills form the only high ground in the Cairo area. From them, there is a panoramic view over the whole city, which extends on both sides of the Nile. Half-way up the hillside is the famous Cairo Citadel. This was built in A.D. 1177 by the great Saracen leader, Saladin. Also on the slopes of the Mokattam Hills is the Mohammed Ali Mosque. It is named after the nineteenth-century ruler of Egypt who built it and was later buried there. Although it is Turkish rather than Egyptian in appearance, the mosque is easily the best-known landmark in Cairo, with its cluster of domes and two very tall, thin minarets.

Most of the modern buildings in Cairo are on the east bank of the Nile. There are also two islands in the river—Gezira and Roda—which include modern residential areas. The old quarter of the city lies between this modern sector and the Mokattam Hills. In recent years, however, Cairo has spread in all directions on both banks of the Nile.

For tourists, one of the most fascinating places in Cairo is the Cairo Museum. For the cost of a small entrance fee, you can see the most wonderful collection of Egyptian antiquities in the world. Apart from countless other treasures, it houses the fabulous finds made in the tomb of King Tutankhamon. There

are rooms full of precious objects, many of them made of gold and encrusted with jewels. Most remarkable of all is the solid gold coffin in which the dead king was buried. It is fashioned to look like the king himself, wearing his royal robes and holding a crook and a flail as a sign of authority. This coffin alone weighs 440 lb. (200 kilograms). It is the largest gold object in existence in the world.

Forty minutes by bus from the centre of Cairo, on the west bank of the Nile, are the famous Pyramids of Giza. They were all built of limestone quarried from the Mokkattam Hills. The Great Pyramid, built by King Cheops, is composed of more than two million blocks of stone, each weighing more than two tons (about 2,540 kilograms). That is, enough to build a wall ten feet (three metres) high, all the way from London to New York.

Only a short distance from the Pyramids is the famous

Sphinx. This is an immense carving of a creature with the body of a lion and the head of a man. It is carved out of one solid piece of natural rock. The Sphinx may have been intended to be the guardian of the temple at the base of one of the Pyramids.

Next to Cairo, the largest and most important city in Egypt is Alexandria. It stands at the mouth of the Nile Delta, and has a population of more than 2,250,000. As well as being an industrial city, Alexandria is also the third largest port in the Mediterranean. Its principal export is the raw cotton which is produced in vast quantities in the Nile Delta.

In the nineteenth century, wealthy travellers often took boat trips up the River Nile. They usually set out from Cairo, and visited such famous towns as Luxor, Aswan and Abu Simbel. All these places are still very popular with sightseers. Nowadays, however, most people reach Luxor and Aswan either by train or by air, and continue their journey to Abu Simbel by hydrofoil.

On the east bank of the Nile at Luxor is the ancient city of Karnak. It has a huge temple to Amon Raa, the most famous of all the ancient Egyptian gods. On the west bank is the incredible Valley of the Kings, where more than sixty pharaohs were buried. It was in this desolate spot that the English archaeologist, Howard Carter, found King Tutankhamon's tomb.

Aswan has been a well known town since very early times. It is at the site of the first cataract on the Nile, and it was once also at the cross-roads of several great caravan routes. Today, tourists like to take trips on the picturesque sailing-boats, called

15278

*feluccas,* and visit the temples on the small islands in the Nile.

Abu Simbel is famous for its gigantic temple cut out of the natural rock. Its façade alone is 108 feet (33 metres) high, and 125 feet (38 metres) wide. Outside it is guarded by four colossal statues of King Ramses II, each 65 feet (20 metres) high. Between the legs of these, there are small statues of the king's family, including his wife, Queen Nefertiti.

When the Aswan High Dam was built the great temple nearly disappeared for ever. It was so close to the Nile that there seemed no way of saving it from being flooded by the water. Fortunately, with the help of experts from all over the world, it was found possible to cut the temple into a number of fairly small pieces and then reassemble them well above the high-water mark.

Between Aswan and the boundary between Egypt and the Sudan lies the region called Nubia. The people here are of mixed Arab and Negro blood, and are mostly very dark-skinned. A large part of Nubia was flooded when the new dam was built, but the majority of the people have now been resettled in other parts of the region.

Nubia is easily the most impoverished area in Egypt. Most of the people are dressed in rags, and their homes are made of beaten earth with roofs of palm-branches or leaves. Usually, the only possessions the Nubians have are their buffaloes. These are used for every purpose, from drawing carts and ploughs to providing the people with milk.

The Arabs in most parts of North Africa are Moslems. In

Egypt, on the other hand, there are approximately 1,500,000 Christian Arabs. These people are members of the ancient Coptic Church. Their church services are simple, and great emphasis is placed on fasting and on reading the Gospels.

Most of the Copts are *fellahin* of the Nile Valley. There are also a great many Coptic churches and monasteries in Cairo. One of the churches, dedicated to St Sergius, is built over the grotto where Mary and Joseph are supposed to have rested with the Infant Jesus during their flight into Egypt.

## *Life in the Desert*

The Sahara covers an area of more than 3,500,000 square miles (9,000,000 square kilometres). There is no other desert in the world that is even half as large as the Sahara. Only a small part of it lies in the countries described in this book. But no account of life in North Africa would be complete without a description of this vast desert.

When we think of a desert we usually picture a burning hot expanse of sand. This is true of very few of the great deserts, and it is certainly not true of the Sahara. Of course, there is sand in the Sahara, and it is sometimes very hot indeed. But this is not the whole story. The Sahara is much more varied and interesting than that.

First, the Sahara is not always fiercely hot. At sunset, for instance, the temperature suddenly falls, and the nights are often bitterly cold. In the daytime, a drop of water falling on a stone would probably sizzle. But, at night, a drop of water falling on the same stone might very well turn to ice!

Secondly, the whole of the Sahara is not a sandy waste. In fact, only about one fifth of the entire desert is covered with sand. This sandy area is known by the Berber name *erg*. Most of the erg is made up of enormous sand-dunes, some of them more than 600 feet (183 metres) high.

Another large area of the Sahara is covered with pebbles and small stones. Hardly a blade of grass grows in this region, and oases are very rare there. This dreary, flat land where nothing lives has the curious name of *reg*.

Then there is the vast rocky plateau called the *hammada*. This covers a greater area of the Sahara than either the erg or the reg. All the soil has been swept away from the hammada by the strong winds which always blow there. It looks rather like the pictures we sometimes see of the surface of the moon!

**Sand-dunes in the desert**

**Sheep grazing in the shade of date palms**

The only green, fertile places in the Sahara are the oases. They are scattered over most parts of the desert, but the distance between them is often enormous. The average oasis has less than one hundred inhabitants. These people are usually Berbers, although in the Fezzan province of Libya they are nearly all Negroes.

Almost every oasis in North Africa is surrounded by tall date palms. They are by far the most important form of vegetation in the Sahara. As a food, dates are rich in fat, sugar and protein. The fibre around the trunks is used to make ropes and matting, while the trunks themselves are used to hold up the flat, clay roofs of the houses.

The palms are also greatly valued for the shade they give. Figs, peaches, oranges, lemons and pomegranates can be grown under their waving fronds. Yet more crops can be planted in the shade of these fruit trees. Wheat, barley, millet, pumpkins and tomatoes all grow well by an oasis.

The people of the oases are not the true desert-dwellers. The real men of the desert are the nomads who live deep in the heart

**A Tuareg musician playing on his pipe, accompanied by women drummers**

of the Sahara. The best known of these wandering people are the curious Tuareg tribes. They are found mainly in Algeria, Libya and the regions that border these countries to the south.

The Tuareg tribesmen are members of the Berber race. They are tall and handsome, with light skins, long black hair and dark eyes. Each tribe has its own prince known as an *Amnukal*. His chief task is to look after his people's interests and to settle any disputes that may arise.

The Tuareg tribesmen are often called "the blue-veiled people of the desert". It is the men of the Tuareg tribes, and not the women, who wear a veil! The veil is indigo blue in colour, and measures about 9 inches by $3\frac{1}{2}$ yards (25 cms. by 3 metres). It is wound round and round the face and neck so that only the eyes are left showing. The rest of the head and neck is covered with an indigo blue turban. Both the veils and the turbans were worn originally as a protection during sandstorms. A Tuareg boy first covers his face on his eighteenth birthday. After that he practically never takes off his veil, even when he is eating or sleeping!

Each of the Tuareg tribes is divided into many much smaller groups. Usually forty or fifty people live together in nine or ten goatskin tents. Inside the tents there is no furniture, except mats and cushions. The women cook out-of-doors, and serve the food in gourds or in roughly made wooden bowls.

The men of the Tuareg tribes are nearly all herdsmen. They keep cows, goats and sheep, as well as donkeys and camels for riding. During the winter they pitch their tents beside an oasis, but in the summer they move on every few days looking for fresh pasture and water for their herds.

Although the Tuareg people are Berbers, they have been living a wandering life for centuries. They think it is shameful for a man to earn his living by tilling the soil. In the past, they were often the robbers and gangsters of the Sahara. Looking rather like modern masked gunmen, they would attack any camel train they saw winding its way across the desert.

The language spoken by the Tuareg tribesmen is called Tamashek. In its written form it must be one of the strangest scripts ever known. It can be written from left to right, like English, or from right to left, like Arabic; but it can also be written from top to bottom, like Chinese, or from bottom to top like no other writing in the world!

## North Africa in the Modern World

North Africa is a land with a history stretching far back into the past. Three thousand years before the birth of Christ, a great civilization had already grown up on the banks of the River Nile. Later, North Africa became in turn the home of the Phoenicians, the Greeks and the Romans. Then, in the eighth century after Christ, it became part of the rapidly expanding Arab empire.

As an Arab land, North Africa reached the height of its glory between the ninth and the fourteenth century after Christ. Even today, the learning and scholarship of the Arabs of this period is reflected in our own everyday lives. Each time we use the figures 0 to 9 we are employing Arabic numerals; and the very words "algebra" and "chemistry" are both derived from the Arabic.

Despite their former greatness, the North African countries began to decline in the fifteenth century after Christ, and for several hundred years they gradually sank into poverty and obscurity. The North Africans generally seemed to accept their position as being "the will of Allah", and made little or no attempt to improve their way of life.

Now, at last, dramatic changes are afoot. All the North

**The River Nile—the key to the earliest civilization in North Africa**

African countries have finally won their independence, and they are eager to take their place in the modern world.

There are, of course, a great many problems to be faced. This is inevitable when any people become independent after many years under the protection of much more powerful nations. Technicians must be recruited; teachers and doctors must be trained; bankers must learn how and where to obtain credit; and politicians must gain experience of international affairs. None of these things can be achieved quickly; but none of them is beyond the powers of a people with the faith in themselves and the ability which the North Africans quite clearly possess.

At the moment, North Africa can best be summed up as a land of contrasts. It is a place where for a time the old and the new can be seen existing side by side. Scribes still sit on the pavement writing letters for people who cannot read or write, but behind them there is often a soaring block of modern offices or flats. Women are still dressed in their voluminous native garments, but underneath they may be wearing the latest creation from a fashion house in Paris.

Before long, no doubt, this situation will come to an end; but for the present it helps to make North Africa one of the world's most exciting and fascinating places.

# *Index*

# *Index*